The Changing Nature of Work – Author's Speaking Topic

By

Richard A. Kaumeyer, Jr.
(Dick Kaumeyer)

Kaumeyer Consulting Group, Inc.

First soft cover edition June 2017

For information about special discounts for bulk purchases, please
contact Richard A. Kaumeyer, Jr. at dkaumeyer@aol.com

Interior design by C. Spencer Reynolds
www.SpencerReynolds.com

Book cover design and layout by Kurt Michelson
info@thewordkurt.com

ISBN-10: 1547282215
ISBN-13: 978-1547282210

Contents

Introduction

The topic of this book is one the writer has addressed for more than three decades. The size of the audience has ranged from a couple of dozen to around three thousand. Things do not remain constant and certainly have changed throughout time. Those who keep current are often able to not only address personal needs, but those of the organization they work for or own.

 In addition to this, the writer has facilitated one of the most highly recognized networking groups in the Los Angeles area for more than eighteen years. This group reaches out to the community with a wide range of current topics of interest. Also, he has been able to bring in some of the best local speakers to address these issues. These are a few of the reasons for his extremely high rating.

Dedication

This book is dedicated to Carol, my wonderful wife, who helped on the initial typing and creation of the manuscript. We have been married for over fifty-four years. It is also dedicated to my son, Rick. Also, to my son, Jon, who is the father of our three wonderful grandchildren.

Chapter 1
Changes On All Fronts

Not only do people come and go in today's job market, but so do companies. Thirty years ago people still joined companies and planned to stay until they retired. Anyone with this philosophy today is programming themselves for serious trouble and career disaster.

Having worked in outplacement (sometimes called career transition assistance) for decades and having owned a retained executive search firm, one gets a different perspective. Everything is in a constant state of change and the change is exponential rather than arithmetic.

I have talked with many individuals who seem to be on a career rocket to success. They have just been named employee or executive of the year. Their picture and award plaque hangs proudly displayed in a prominent place in the corporation. Their relationship with their boss, peers, and subordinates is fantastic. Recently, they have received one of the highest salary increases and corporate bonuses ever given out. Life at their work is a dream come true.

This is only the beginning of the story heard repeatedly.

This same charmed individual, let's say his name is John. He is in his car a few weeks later casually listening to the news on a local radio station, as he is driving to his wonderful job.

The business section of the news comes on and he hears his company is considering an offer from another firm. A month later the acquisition takes place. Three months later John is reporting to someone from the new owner's company. The new boss calls John in and says he is being replaced with a colleague the new boss worked with at another company several years ago.

This wonderful work life completely changes in a matter of a few months.

The interesting part of this happening is that the change has nothing to do with the individual's ability, productivity, dedication, or any other measurable contribution.

 All the work, worry, and long hours had nothing to do with the loss of the much loved and valuable job. The circumstances affecting this change are completely out of the involved individual's control. This is not an isolated or rare occurrence and happens to thousands of people each week and has happened to the author.

What is really occurring in today's economy and our current world where we work? Decades ago long-term and short-term planning were in the five-year range. At the same time, people went to work for a company assuming they would be there for their entire career.

Only the risk-takers assumed they would work for possibly a second company. Those with three or more companies on their resume were considered "job hoppers" and no one aspired to having this title.

Corporations fit this pattern and their planning was based on long-term horizons. Many corporate plans and strategies were based on positioning for long-term results. These were done based on reaping benefits many years in the future and possibly losing value (money) for several years to do this.

Corporate institutions don't take this approach in today's world. In many cases, the planning cycle is very, very short. Long-term planning is often no more than the end of the quarter and short-term planning the end of the month.

Companies that are publically traded and don't follow this rule may have their stock trashed if they veer in another direction. We often see companies even taken private, if there are major short-term expenses that can't be avoided.

The same concepts often apply to startups. We have talked to numerous people in the process of starting companies and no one seems to be reaching out for decades. In fact, what is often heard is the intent to get a company quickly up and running with an almost immediate profit. This has to be, since long-term funding is almost non-existent.

Having talked with several people in a start-up mode, there seems to be a pattern. Many want to get the company up, running, and showing an immediate profit. The goal is often to rapidly position it in the marketplace within two to three years and then for the originator to cash out. This can be through a direct sale or a rapid IPO. This seems to be a very real goal on many fronts in today's world.

In talking with a wide range of executives throughout the years, there is a greater effect than just the loss of jobs and the transfer of work out of the country. It becomes difficult, if not impossible, to control ownership of the product or proprietary information related to the product or activity once it leaves U.S. shores. Most people in the know will tell you that within eighteen months to two years ownership is often compromised. New companies in foreign names, with new names, frequently start producing the same product or service. This is often at an even cheaper price and sometimes results in a total loss for the originator.

Many people feel it is only products that are outsourced, but we have seen it affect every aspect of life. Just out of curiosity we started asking friends their company's corporate location and quickly found they can be across the globe.

Even going to one's local doctor or hospital quickly causes this function to be activated. Tests that are run are sometimes zapped to experts in other countries. The results are analyzed and zapped back where the patient is and then given by the attending physician.

The cost savings are the drivers of this activity be they a product or service. Off-shoring can often result in savings of 90 or more percent versus doing it locally. Also, in many cases the technical expertise and training of those involved are often much higher and better than what is available locally.

Education varies by country and some of the technical leadership follows. For decades, the United States has had many college students focusing on majors in education, psychology, history, and other non-science subjects. Simultaneously, vast numbers of people in Germany, India, China, and other countries are focused on studying math and other sciences. Organizations are often forced to go where the knowledge they need for their product or service exists.

Demographics and the general makeup of the workforce can have some significant effects on the economy. We have all heard about Japan's aging workforce and the tremendous effect it has had on their economy. There are large numbers of people aging and retiring with fewer people in the more recent generations to take their place.

A similar situation is in process in the United States—the "Boomer Generation" that resulted in a major social shift in the country during the later part of the 1960s, 1970s, and part of the 1980s. They are the people born between 1946 and 1964—the generation that in their teens and early twenties were noted for "sex, drugs, and rock and roll." This is often stated, but may be more of a joke than reality. They are the product of the WWII generation— those who postponed major family growth due to the Depression and then the war. When it ended and families reunited, the birthrate exploded as those involved in the war effort changed their focus to a peace-time economy. They rebuilt their lives, education, and work focus.

Large families were created and became almost a social requirement. The explosion continued until the early 1960s and was then somewhat slowed with the advent of the birth control pill. The number in the Boomer Generation is often estimated as as being 75 to 80 million people, depending on whose statistics you look at.

Also, the economic underpinning was supportive of this massive growth. WWII had severely damaged, if not totally obliterated, the major industrial centers in Europe and in Asia. Simultaneously, it left the US economic centers, not only untouched, but built for growth and continued expansion.

The damage done in Europe and Asia produced ready markets for just about every conceivable product. This continued as almost everything had to be rebuilt from scratch. This was not a one-time or quick process, but took many decades and provided the United States with a huge market on an ongoing basis.

The economy provided a steady stream of high-paying jobs. Companies grew and expanded at an unprecedented rate. The "cold war" with Russia and China assured that defense and military spending, which briefly slowed at the end of WWII, would continue.

The growing families and relatively secure economy further created an explosion in city and suburban growth. The norm was to keep moving upward in a company and upgrading one's housing. To say the Boomer Generation was born in a time of plenty would be an understatement. Of course, this same environment led the group in a new social direction.

 As previously mentioned, the advent of the birth control pill in 1964 effectively influenced future growth. This caused a population drop and only about forty million people were added during the next several decades often referred as "Generation X."

Beginning in 2011 those in the Boomer Generation started turning sixty-five according to some reports. In fact, most statisticians say there are ten thousand people a day reaching this age. Needless to say, this creates some interesting changes in our society. This is one of the age areas that has been a target for some people for retirement and some say it is supported by it being around the time Medicare health coverage becomes available. Of course this varies significantly depending on the person.

One factor that is seldom discussed is the health of people as they enter into their later years. The statistics in this area can vary widely depending on the source. In the author's family, very few people were able to continue working with no limitations past sixty. In fact, a few were not able to continue to work at all. This said, looking back historically the author's great-grandfather worked past eighty, and his grandfather worked up until he died just a few months shy of ninety-two.

What does this tell us? The relationship between the aging

population and the dramatic affect on the workforce may be greater than the credit it is given. Much of the writing on the topic indicates life expectancy is increasing, so people will be able to work longer.

The magic target of mid sixties and beyond is always under consideration for extension. This includes the date to start being fully qualified for Social Security continues to be extended. This blindly assumes that all of those reaching this age can automatically just continue working their (assumed) normal eight to ten hour days (including commute). What if this isn't true for everyone? Could it be that a certain percent of the population may cease to be able to participate in the workforce due to physical considerations? Yes, they may be living longer than their predecessors, but can they still actively work in a corporate environment at the necessary pace? The author himself is well into his seventies and continues to work full time plus. I am sure there are a large number of people who are in this category.

We certainly have new medical techniques and drugs that allow people to live longer. Does this longer life really mean a "longer working life"? Heaven knows, most people want, and many financially need to work into their seventies, eighties, nineties, and possibly even longer, but how many really can? The author is in his late seventies and continues to put in full weeks and more. Many of these consist of sixty or more hours. Is everyone this fortunate?

Chapter 2
We Are All Self-Employed

Two or three decades ago people used to go to a company or organization, and planned on staying. In fact, having more than three companies a person worked for on his or her resume could be considered negative. This was sometimes waived if the person was going to school while holding a position.

 The author had a related experience while on a speaking assignment. This occurred in the early 1980s and was with a Rotary group who were in second careers. These were all "C Level" executives who had sold their company early, retired, and decided to then come back to work in the corporate environment.

The author had more than forty-five very polished (probably wealthy) executives in the room. The topic they wanted discussed was should a person stay with one company for an entire career, maybe two and, if I wanted to push the envelope, possibly three.

In starting my speech I mentioned I would, in the next several years, have children looking at going to college.

I mentioned that in counseling them and looking out ten years or more, it would be difficult to even identify a current local company that would even exist. This was very true, but the mention of this to this group was a huge mistake.

You would have thought I slapped my mother, burnt the flag, and stepped in the apple pie. They literally went ballistic! Many shouted out the names of existing large local companies (they no longer exist) and asked if I were stupid enough to believe they would go away. Many started shaking their fists and shouting obscenities. One even called me a G.D. Communist bastard to even talk like this. In an attempt to avoid a riot (or worse) I reminded the group that I had been an Air Force officer, served the country, and had held one of the highest security clearances. This did have a little calming effect, but gaining back any form of trust was out of the question. Anyone who does a lot of public speaking has a number of horror stories to share. This one is somewhat unique in that it shows just how far off base even the most senior executives can be when confronted with facts that are contrary to their training and belief system.

This really brings into question our leadership structure and who the "experts" actually are. If financially successful executives, who have run major business enterprises can't face change, on whom can we trust and depend?

When the facts the author was so thoroughly condemned for all turned out to be correct, a major gap occurred. I soon learned that maybe one is better off being one's own expert rather than depend on those society has established as experts.

This is not only true in the business world, but may or not be true in one's personal financial management as well. Occasionally people with financial advisors are sometimes losing, if not being totally wiped out, with each financial hiccup, recession, or depression (the forbidden word).

The author and a few friends may have made finance/business a hobby, since their early years. This doesn't mean a few quick seminars or reading a few books, but hundreds/thousands of hours throughout the decades of playing with the topics one hour or two a week as time permitted.

As your own financial advisor, you can draw conclusions and commit money based on what you have learned. You are not focused on promoting products from companies who pay you a commission. You have only your success or failure to focus on and that is your only pay. The author is far from being rich, but has often been able to avoid the major market collapses. This said, he has possibly been too conservative and missed real opportunities.

Some will counter and say, "Then hire a 'fee-only advisor.' " The counter to this might be how many clients with widely varied needs and portfolios do they have to balance? If they have too many clients, can't these cause problems of focus and delivery for you? However, there is probably value for many in having someone with this level of experience. For those who don't like to manage their own finances, selecting someone after doing significant research may be of value whether the person works on a commission or a fee basis. The author might have become wealthy if he had done this or listened to his wife on certain occasions. Instead he has to still work to survive.

Now, if you have spent thousands of hours throughout the years focusing on you, and no one else, it can make a difference. You're not worried about commissions or having a large client base to bring in fees. Your only concern is to continue to gain knowledge and focus on only your own money concerns.

The reason for this investment analogy is to get back to executives in a work environment. The ones described earlier couldn't "see the forest for the trees," since the companies they knew were their only source of income. The mere mention that their firm might not be there in a decade was not acceptable, even though the prediction was valid and eventually was fulfilled. We are truly always in a learning mode, whether it is inventory/income related or job/income related. Those who don't continue to learn and adjust accordingly don't survive.

If you talk to a number of recruiters or outplacement consultants, they will tell you that the time most people spend at a company is presently an average of less than three or four years. Some will tell you it is often less than two. This is a far cry from most people's hopes and dreams. As a search firm owner, I almost fall off my chair when I see someone who has been at a company ten or more years. This also calls into question the level of interest my client may have in this person, since his or her experience is very parochial.

What used to be considered job hopping is now considered the norm. The person (or employee) may be stronger for it. Each company or organization has its own personality. People who move learn quickly to adapt and be flexible on many different issues, if they are going to quickly fit in and be productive in the new environment.

Technology and world markets are in a state of rapid change and development. Organizations and people have to be as well. It is often said that if you do happen to stay with a company for five years and it remains successful, it won't be the same company you started with. Could it also be true that if you survived that long, you too will be a somewhat different person from a work and skill-set perspective?

In today's world you constantly have to be aware of the changes and become part of them if you are going to survive. This is changing everything including the education system itself. The concept of going to a classic four-year college and coming out ready to enter the workforce may be in a state of change also. It is often said that things learned as a freshman are obsolete by the time someone is a junior or senior. Could it be that if there is value today in this experience it comes from the social contacts one makes and not the knowledge?

In the workplace, who is responsible for your next job? Is it the employer, a mentor, yourself, or someone else? In some cases the answers are all of the above, plus some additional possibilities. Employers sometimes try for retention of top performers and make efforts to do this. Executive mentors try to help people develop and this sometimes leads to their referring people to positions outside the current structure or company.

It is a wise person who recognizes that he or she is today operating in a chaotic environment. Job knowledge is obviously a very important component in keeping a current position and finding the next one. Those considered in the top 5 percent of their career field usually are able to find positions even in terrible economic times. In good times, it is usually the top 20 percent who can find positions with very little effort.

Staying current can be a bit of a challenge since it often requires strong involvement in professional organizations. It also requires regular attendance at some of the training seminars most professional groups offer to their members. These often cost the members both time and money (if not company reimbursed), but are usually more than worth it.

These training sessions are invaluable, not only for the information and knowledge updates, but most important for the contacts one makes at these sessions. Always try to go away with five or six business cards of colleagues in your field who are attending and always take the card of the instructor or instructors. Immediately label them as to date, topic, and so on and keep them where they can be easily retrieved, even after leaving your current employer. This allows you ready access to future technical answers by a quick call or e-mail to the person, prefaced by stating how you met. You are never going to leave a professional group training session with all of the answers, but having these contacts will quickly get them for you 95 percent of the time.

Also, I mentioned being in the top of one's field. Always remember the old adage: "an ounce of image is worth a pound of performance." One of the best ways to do this is to become a speaker on a topic that is dear to you in your field. If you are nervous about speaking, join Toastmasters and get over it. Speaking on topics in one's field is the fastest way to raise one's image to the top of the heap in a person's profession. This not only raises how you are viewed by fellow professionals, but others in your company who don't know, or possibly even understand, what you do.

There is no better way to raise your image in a company than to have your absence noted because you are out that day speaking. People automatically upgrade their perception of you when they find you are speaking about topics in your career field. Once you are on the agenda somewhere to speak, it is quite easy to circulate an e-mail to others and even to anonymously post on the company's bulletin board.

This is just a start to raise your visibility. Communicating in the written mode is another. It used to be that the way to do this was through writing professional articles and/or books. Technology has expanded this further into blogs, tweets, and a wide range of professional posts on business and group membership sites. This can be used not only to share and improve your image, but to also engage contacts in your network and to learn in a very rapidly changing environment.

Chapter 3
The New Worker

Preparing to enter the labor force at one time was a rather clear-cut, structured process. One received training in technical schools or, in some cases, started and was trained on the job in the blue collar arena. Those aspiring to professional management positions usually went to colleges or universities to get a degree and then went to a company that had openings in their chosen field and were trained/mentored in their career field.

Just having a degree in about any field allowed one to enter the workforce at a professional level. Many people selected broad, less strenuous fields of study such as history, psychology, sociology, and so on. This made it easier for those who did not want to deal with math and science topics.

Those who were comfortable in the math/science arena were somewhat few in number. This allowed those majoring in engineering, physics, and so on to often start at an even higher professional salary in most workplaces throughout the country.

Those moving on to higher degrees, such as masters or doctorates in either math or non-math oriented majors were often brought onboard at a higher salary. This was based on the assumption that they had already proven themselves to be outstanding performers.

In the retained search area it has been interesting watching the changes that have happened and are continuing to happen regarding hiring and education. Hiring officers tend to want to hire in their own image. If they have a technical degree, they want to hire someone with the same. If they have an advanced degree, this may be something they are more apt to want to hire. The opposite can also occur, and people with a lesser degree may feel threatened or prefer to hire people with a similar background.

In the business world, a doctorate degree in the 1970s and 1980s almost guaranteed a higher-paying professional job. This has about totally reversed from the 1990s forward. Having a doctorate sometimes can make finding a job in the corporate world difficult.

With the exception of companies engaged in areas of specific technical research, some may not talk to someone with a doctorate. The feeling in the corporate world is someone with this background is going to over-analyze and slow the decision-making process. There is also the feeling that someone who has reached this level will look down on his or her peers, superiors, and subordinates who don't have an advanced degree.

The situation is sometimes so difficult that many people who hold doctorates and are looking for a corporate job won't even show it on their resume. We have seen a few instances where they only reveal it on the job application when a position is being offered.

This gets back to the point made earlier, that possibly our entire college/university system is outdated. Things are changing at an ever-increasing rate. When someone's training as a college freshman is obsolete by the time he or she is a junior or senior, this tends to speak for itself.

This situation brings into question what value is a college education to the business world? If it has helped people to organize their thinking or allows them to be better report writers, might there be better systems to do this?

The author was singled out during officers' training in the military because he gave totally different and more accurate answers to hypothetical questions posed about specific management actions. The instructor wanted to know if he got this more accurate and practical training from the well-known university he attended. The answer was "No" — he had received the training by working many years as a night manager in a restaurant during college, where most of the workers were ex-convicts who were ten to twenty years his senior. He was put in the management position responsible for money, staff, and other items of value because he had not done time in prison. The learning was trial and error throughout the years, but it was not the classic management book learning of the time.

The traditional four-year college education may be coming to an end for a wide range of reasons. The item just posed may be only minor, as too many people have been brought up to believe in its value whether it is proved or not.

There are much greater influences that may work to change their value. One is cost and it seems to be increasing at a geometric rate. The decades of overspending by both individual and government agencies are starting to take a toll. It used to be high college costs were primarily in the domain of the well-regarded private colleges. Today, state and local government colleges are raising rates at an extremely rapid pace due to huge government deficits, staff pensions, and decrease in revenue.

Many people can no longer afford the cost unless their company sponsors them or borrow the money. Corporations are now almost all trying to cut costs and this is one of their major targets. If an individual can qualify for a loan, it can quickly become a huge debt burden. Not only is it a burden, but one that cannot be discharged in bankruptcy. In essence it follows the person until it is fully paid. Does this risk result in a true value?

Another factor is the changing way we learn to communicate. Will the college of the future be online and not made of bricks and mortar? More and more colleges are offering online opportunity for at least some, if not all of their courses. What effect will this have on people's social interactions and future business connections and networking? These contacts are a major focus and value to some of the most successful people.

Traditionally, universities at the top of the list are: Harvard, Yale, Princeton, Stanford, Northwestern, Rice, Vanderbilt, and so on. People certainly get instructors of the highest quality possible, but is this where all the value comes? I wonder if the contacts are actually the most valuable part of the experience. Those attending are in constant contact, they establish relationships, and become close friends with people whose families lead the world. They are the leaders in politics, corporations, and financial acumen. In the future, these contacts can often "move mountains," by nothing more than making a single phone call.

What happens to these valued relationships in an online world? This is a question I am not sure anyone truly has an answer for. The entire concept of online learning and education is just starting to affect the world of formal schooling. The true results and/or consequences are yet to be known, only guessed. It may take a while for this to sort itself out. The only thing we know for sure is there is an increasing effect on all aspects of life as it continues to rapidly unfold.

Re-entering the workforce after a period of absence is another item of change. We have had this issue for some time, since people leave for periods of time for a wide variety of reasons and then return after a period of a year to a decade. One of the most often, most visible, and most discussed is leaving to have and care for children. Many generations ago women were homemakers and often, with few exceptions, not major players in the workplace. With the advent of significantly effective birth control that became available in the mid 1960s a significant change was created. This truly gave women the freedom to become active participants in the workforce, with the ability to take advantage of professional career opportunities. Along with this are the efforts by most of us to avoid any type of job-related discrimination.

Today, many select when and the number of children they will have and directly relate their business careers to this choice. There are significant numbers who want to drop out of the labor force for a period of time while their children are younger and not yet in school to be with them during this very formative period. It can often be for a significant number of years. Today, many men are selecting the option of being a stay-at-home dad; things are changing. Men in today's world truly share in the issues previously mentioned and this is a very positive change.

Yes, there are other reasons people temporarily leave the labor force such as health issues or attempts to retire early. Yet, one of the most significant reasons across the board still seems to be related to the family issue.

What is involved in getting back to work after an absence of several years? Today, there are probably a lot more than many expect. There are many issues that influence this and almost all are related to the series of rapid changes taking place in today's working world.

As was pointed out earlier, if one has stayed with a company for five years or more, it will be a totally different company than when one joined. Rapid product obsolesce, combined with the same in corporate technology create an entirely new corporation in a very short period of time.

People who re-enter the workforce after a period of years must step back and do a detailed evaluation of their skill set versus what is being done now. In many cases, extensive training may be required. This assumes that the prior job function even still exists. Many people may require professional help to do this.

The leading edge of this is how technology is changing the way we work. Things that used to be mailed through the post office are now sent electronically such as by way of e-mail, tweets, Skype, and instant messaging. These are leading to a wide range of other changes including office locations and travel.

More and more people are working part-time, if not full-time, from home or wherever they are when needed. The days of going to a commercial building with hundreds of "cubicle monkeys" running around is rapidly coming to an end.

Travel itself is not only costly, but has become more dangerous and the counter security measures make it more difficult and less enjoyable. Do we have to fly people in just to have a meeting? With the availability of modern teleconferencing technologies, this may no longer be the necessity it once was.

How this will change the ways we socially interact with coworkers is becoming a real question. What about the business relationships that develop when people physically meet together, go out for lunch or dinner? Sometimes these are more valuable than the actual meetings themselves, but now they have to be replaced because the way we communicate and share with each other is changing.

Chapter 4
The Established Worker

We just discussed the rapid changes that are taking place in the business world. These changes are coming at us so rapidly, it brings into question our entire learning system and the various colleges many of us want to attend. To many people, even the mention of this is terrifying. What about not going to a four-year college because it has outlived its value? How does one even suggest such a thing!

Take just a minute and reflect on how you use today's cell phone and computer. Many professionals dread (some are secretly happy) being on an airplane for business travel, or just travel of any type. For a period of time all phones and computers must be shut down in order not to interfere with the plane's communication and controls.

This too is changing and possibly by the time this book is printed new technology will have solved this problem. Then you will have no escape, even for a few hours, from talking and working. This is one of the reasons continued learning is ongoing, important, and ever changing. Just about the time you have mastered your latest communication device, a new and different one comes onto the market. It used to be that technology changed every eighteen months and now it seems it is about every six months.

This has a wide range of implications in the business world, and not the least of these is the cost/investment. What is the optimum time to convert to the latest technology that is truly cost effective? This is a real issue and, unfortunately, it is probably not being taught in most of today's business schools.

Most of the people the author knows are "flying by the seat of their pants" on this issue. There are certain professions where one has to have the latest technology if they are to work there and be accepted. In many others, it is a matter of individual choice, drive, and the ultimate cost decision.

As was noted earlier, companies are coming and going exponentially rather than at an arithmetic rate. A person's company and the people they work with can easily become an extended family. To some, they are the entire family. The rate of change in the business world is affecting this as well.

One's network has always been important. It now may be the most important thing one has in today's business world. Very few people stay very long at a company, even if they wish to. Jobs are constantly shifting as companies outsource, move off-shore, merge, and are sold. It is hard to even be at one place for two or three years as today's economy shifts.

One major company the writer has dealt with transferred a large portion of its finance activities to a country in South America, another has sent most of its manufacturing to Mexico and closed/sold local buildings where it was once located.

A major recruiting firm in the hospital/medical industry recently opened an office in India. Why? Many of their hospital clients now take patient monitor readings, lab tests, and more and zap them via the Internet to doctors in other countries where the detailed analysis is done and sent back to the hospital. The results and findings are then given to the patient via the hospital's medical staff without the patient even knowing who did what or where it was done.

Bricks and mortar no longer support where work is done and by whom. One person I know well who works in computer technology for a major corporation, gets up at 4:00 a.m. on the West Coast, so they can deal with counterparts on the East Coast as they start their work day.

They often take a nap around the time it would be lunch on the East Coast and then continue working until quitting time there. This becomes even more complex when a person is working on both coasts for a company with offices in both places. Complex, yes, but with a home office and the disappearance of brick and mortar, successful people are learning how to deal with it. Technology and the changing nature of work are in an ongoing state of flux in today's business world. This gets even more complex when a person is dealing with other countries in Europe, Asia, etc.

It used to be that where one worked tended to define one and, to some extent, one's life. It may now be one's network that fits this model. Jobs and companies are rapidly coming and going; so also is knowledge and technology. It may be that the people one knows and stays in touch with have replaced more traditional relationships.

People's work colleagues used to be a second family and, for some, their family. People could put in long days, weekends, forgo vacations, and holidays, yet they were with people who meant a tremendous amount in all aspects of their lives. Many people just went to work, kept their contacts with only their work colleagues and, for all intents and purposes, were totally unknown outside of their company and sometimes even their departments. Their entire career and life centered in this relationship. Boy, has this changed today, and many people can't adapt to it. Losing their job, having their company sold/merged, the closing of their facility, and other job changes happen now to almost everyone. It is no longer a rare or one-time occurrence, but happens repeatedly at an ever-increasing rate.

This is why changing work-related behavior is so important. To survive and succeed in today's world you must have a strong network, maybe in your career field, but certainly outside of your company. Yes, you have to put in so many hours to keep your job and do well in your job, but it is only temporary. It is temporary at an ever increasing rate. Someone with a company longer than three years is often now considered an "old timer."

One rule of thumb is for every eight hours you put in for the company, you should put in hour for yourself. This hour for yourself can be on company time, but if handled right, it can be of joint value or non-visible. Meetings, phone calls, lunches with suppliers and vendors are present and future contacts. Attending professional meetings and conferences with people from other companies is extremely valuable. Accepting professional speaking engagements outside of the company can be priceless.

Calls, e-mails, lunches, drinks, etc., with these outside con-tacts should be done as often as possible. Collect business cards, phone numbers, and e-mail addresses, and develop relationships on social media such as LinkedIn and Facebook. Keep copies of all of these on your personal cell, laptop, etc. and protect by your personal cloud service. They are so valuable that some might even keep copies in their safe or safety deposit box in case of a major disaster. You certainly don't want to have everything at work. When terminating/laying off an employee, many companies require the person to leave business contact information behind and then immediately block company computer access.

The old days of cradle-to-grave corporate relationships are over! You are your own corporation whether you like it or not. The only loyalty you have in today's world is to yourself. To a company you are nothing more than an expense to be cut whenever necessary.

Those viewed in the top 10 to 20 percent of their current profession seem to find another job more quickly when the axe falls. How do you get into this upper percent category? This is a marketing role. Remember the old adage, "An ounce of image is worth a pound of performance." First, you have to be proactive and go after it. The target is to be visible to the people outside of your company. This is done not only by memberships in outside professional organizations, but by activities such as public speaking, teaching, taking courses, writing article/blogs, and tweets.

You have to be in front of the outside world all of the time. If you fear public speaking (we all do), join Toastmasters or a related organization and conquer it. The time to prepare for your next job is when you are working. The more you control this aspect of today's working world, the greater the opportunity to not only survive, but to succeed!

One mistake is to constantly go to lunch, coffee, drinks, and other gatherings with the colleagues you currently work with. Honestly, the better choice is to socialize with colleagues who have been laid off, fired, or otherwise terminated. These are people you immediately want to find out whether they have landed a new position or not. In fact, it may be better to get to them before they are in a new position, since this is when they are the most vulnerable and able to be reached.

People tend to remember those who helped them when they were unemployed. Not all, but some will try to return the favor when your turn comes to look for a new position. People who are working in today's world are often doing the job of two or three people, since companies cut staff; but the work doesn't go away, it is just redistributed. Those who are between jobs are much easier to reach, since they are not currently buried in work.

Those in transition are not only easier to reach, but will

more than likely have the time to let you get to know them better. There are many advantages to this, including getting access to their friends and others in their networks at a time when they are very willing to share. You can often access people two or three levels above your current position when they are in the job market. This opportunity may close to some degree or even go away completely when the person finds a new position.

Will everyone you reach out to be there for you after they have landed? Normally, the answer is "No!" In fact, it is usually a very small percentage. The answer may be to reach out and help everyone you can, but don't assume they are going to be there when you need them. Almost everyone is surprised because the people they thought would help them don't and those they least expected to help do.

It is said repeatedly, "You find out who your friends really are when you are out of work and reaching out to your network." It is actually a major sorting out process that amazes most of us. This is why most good career counselors employ the "two foot rule." Its basic premise is that when you are between jobs, tell everyone within two feet of you that you are in the job market and looking for work; this is the most rapid route to success.

More people have found their next position through someone at their dry cleaners, barbers, manicurists, and other people they encounter frequently than through formal search channels. It has been often very accurately stated that more people have been placed by their golf caddies than by all of the executive search firms put together!

Chapter 5
The Mature Worker

Supposedly, the Baby Boomers started turning sixty five in the United States in January of 2011, but this (like many statistics) maybe on target or not. This number, according to many statistical experts, accounts for about ten thousand a day. Of course, this causes a great deal of government concern because as people age they can go on Medicare. This might reduce the number on regular insurance and can increase overall government insurance costs.

This number has been changed throughout the years. When social security in the United States first came into being in 1936, only one in four people lived to sixty-five. Also, there were dollar payments at this time, but not health coverage, which now exists through Medicare. This provision was instituted decades later. Today, the life expectancy is much greater—somewhere in the late seventies or early eighties depending on whose statistics you use.

Trying to get accurate information in this area is difficult, to say the least. In some cases, even addressing the issue is difficult because everyone is "tip toeing" around issues where statistics are hard to find. Then you add a host of people in the financial/investment world who are trying to make a buck off retirement concerns and you have one huge, complex issue to try and address.

One thing that many suggest is that people could and should continue working into their later years. Many of us need to keep working and I personally hope my health will allow me to do so. I keep very active and do a ton of walking, as my doctors recommend.

In the author's family a relatively small portion of the close relatives were even able to continue regular work past sixty. In many cases, the illnesses that resulted in the loss of life sometimes restricted the ability of the survivors to continue working. This said, as mentioned earlier, there were grandparents and a great-grandparent who worked well into their eighties and nineties. It is doubtful that anyone knows the real answers to questions in this area. The author himself is in this category and continues to work into his late seventies (often 10 hour days).

This flies in the face of the economists and people's savings, spending, and retirement planning. The idea that people can just go on and work as long as they need or want to is not often realistic. In fact, some careers are ended in the years before sixty. The exact figures in this area are hard to come by, but it certainly may be a significant number. Remember that health and life insurance companies always seem to raise rates as people age. Now, if this is "age discrimination" why are life and medical insurance companies allowed to charge higher rates, or exclude people completely? They do this every day and without any penalties for discrimination. Why? The answer is they have the statistics to back it up. People are more prone to illness and even death as they age and the immune system ceases to function properly.

How many people even have the health to keep working past seventy is a very real question. Some statistics show an ever increasing number work up to, during and beyond their seventies. Whether this is a true number or not is questionable. How much of this is personal desire and how much is health related is an interesting question. The author himself certainly fits into this category.

Taking health and personal interest into consideration there are many, many models for working, and retiring later in your senior years. Your primary consideration is whether you are truly doing what you love to do. People who love their work probably do not want to stop. In some instances, a sit-down-do-nothing retirement may actually speed up the aging/dying process. Who knows the real answer?

The opposite may be true for those who dislike what they do. Most who dislike what they do often work solely for economic purposes. This number may be a lot higher than what many perceive. Regardless of age, many analyses show that a high percentage of those in the workforce don't like their current position/company.

This has some interesting possibilities. If so many people don't like what they do should there be more effort to get people into jobs they like? Of course, the question is when? It may be almost impossible for most people who have young families and significant financial responsibilities. There are periods in most people's lives, excluding the very rich, when the amount of income is more important than happiness.

We have limited training or encouragement to change into companies we love until the monetary stress eases. Most of the people the author knows don't contemplate this until they are going into some form of retirement. When this is money motivated, they don't have enough money coming in to meet their basic needs, the target usually doesn't include work-related pleasures. It is doing something to bring in the needed money whether they enjoy doing it or not. Money, throughout most people's normal working lives and even into retirement years, usually dictates what is done.

Age discrimination is often a worry for everyone. This includes those who have to work in later years for financial reasons as well as those who enjoy what they are doing and don't want to stop. This can be a hard situation for an individual to control if he or she is in the traditional corporate world.

The obvious and the one most often mentioned is ownership—either having significantly bought into a company or starting one to be able to continue to work. There is a whole range of considerations in this option. One of them is financial risk. Ownership or part-ownership of the company assumes the company will do well and prosper. If it doesn't, what is the personal liability of the persons involved? If they are working for financial need reasons, they are even more vulnerable when the company does not perform as desired. If they are doing it because they like the work, are they possibly even risking their secured "nest egg"?

One possible solution in spreading the risk is to pursue what is referred to as portfolio work. The concept is working only one or maybe two days a week with a single business entity. A person could work on Monday only for corporation X and then on Wednesday for corporation Y. The person could then not work, be a consultant, or work at other companies on Tuesdays, Thursdays, and Fridays.

This will depend on the individual's financial needs and personal desire to work.

Portfolio work is becoming more popular among hiring companies, since they may need only a limited amount of one's skill set. This arrangement is starting to be seen as a "win-win" for both companies and people. With skills and corporations coming and going, it may become the wave of the future.

Each individual has to take a step back and analyze his or her own work needs and how much the person is able to deal with the entrepreneurial aspects of today's business world. The days of going with a company and spending all of one's working life there are certainly over. In fact, spending three to five years with the same company is exceptional.

Now, assuming one wishes to become a portfolio worker or just negotiate to a limited amount of work that fits one's schedule, how does one go about doing this? This refers to the subject mentioned earlier of having a network. The network has to include people where one works as well as people outside. The larger the network, the better opportunity for success.

If you are currently with a company and are thinking about

cutting back, talk to someone in power whom you trust. Many company leaders are willing to structure a day or two a week for someone they know rather than trying to replace that person completely. This can be a win-win situation and a good way to either cut back or truly become a portfolio worker with this being your start. Other days can be filled with more companies over time.

Professional organizations are wonderful resources to find portfolio prospects. Those you are networking with here know the field you are in very well and if you have been a contributor over time, they know you. This is a good reason why you belong to such groups—to pursue and accept positions with the group such as; program manager, vice president, president, and others. This enhances not only your leadership skills, but your visibility.

Professional groups attract people from the same field and you can network with a wide range of people regarding the portfolio work you are seeking. It is not unusual for a senior member of the group who works for another company to reach out and offer you a day or two with him or her. In other cases, members have been approached by small companies needing limited service, but they can't accept because of personal or financial needs. This may be a wonderful opportunity for the portfolio worker.

Another major resource is the speakers who come to the group to make presentations. They obviously have connections and a good reputation or they would not have been brought in to speak. In most groups all speakers have to be approved by a group board or at least more than one key member before they get the nod to speak.

Obviously, the meetings are usually not the time to bring up your needs/portfolio targets with speakers. It is a great time to at least meet them and get their contact information. It also gives you a point of reference when reaching out to them. You can quickly explain that you heard them speak, enjoyed it, found it of value, and would like to have coffee with them. Speakers usually do a lot of presentations and are usually very easy to reach out to. Also, many, if not most, have huge networks and are great resources.

One problem portfolio workers can encounter is if one of their one- or two day-a-week clients starts to grow. They may want you to expand the day or days you work for them and often want you to convert to a full-time employee. This can be both good news and bad news depending on your role, their needs, and your objectives.

The good news is they are prosperous and find you of value. The bad news is, depending on your needs/goals, it may interfere with other commitments you have established in your life. There are several ways to approach this and there is always the chance they will go away completely, so be prepared.

In the event you want to keep your current portfolio role, you can tell them so and offer to find a colleague who meets their needs. If you are working two days a week and they want you four or five, offer to find the person to do the additional portfolio work and do any necessary training. This can be appealing, since they already like you and you can more quickly bring a new person up to speed on the corporate culture than they can.

In many companies you can keep your portfolio role by offering to serve on their Advisory Board or even their Corporate Board. This is particularly true if you have held an executive position. These appeal to many companies, especially if you have established yourself as an active networker.

You not only bring your skills to the table, but can reach out to the others for professional information as well as recruiting. This type of contribution can be viewed as invaluable. It also gives you more leverage in protecting and continuing your portfolio status with them. It can also provide additional compensation depending on how it is structured.

Chapter 6
Using Career Counselors and Search Firms

What if you don't know where to start? What if you aren't sure about your future? Want if you don't know what you really want to be in your later years?

Again, finding the answers can be difficult and sometimes very costly. This is another instance where having a large network and memberships in a number of professional organizations will pay off. This is an area where you want to be cautious, since there are charlatans out there. These are people who may be looking to get your money and not much else.

One of the first steps is rather obvious. We all know people who love what they do and are working very successfully past an age and stage where others have quit. Ask them about why and how they are doing and what they are doing? Did they get professional help? Counseling? Testing? If so, by whom, and would they do it again? If they had to pay, how much would they pay and would they recommend this resource?

Check with your network and leaders of your professional

organizations whom you respect. This is an area where you truly want to take your time and do in-depth research. Interview those who are recommended at length. Talk to all of their references.

Will your company consider paying for this? This is a question many people forget to ask when it looks as though their company is going to go away or terminate employment relationships. Many executives actually have outplacement/career transition services written into their employment agreement. Usually, if it is a company-sponsored program, there is an agreement with a pre-selected outplace/career transition company. This is not necessarily set in stone. Often, the company will allow the person leaving to make another selection as long as the price/fee for the counseling service/consultant is the same. Many counselors/consultants in this area are open to a new client's fee, based on the competition in the market.

Knowing the current market is very important. Normally, a recession or downturn in the economy is not a good time to be looking for a new job. It is usually a horrible time for a career change. Those doing the hiring are often able to pick and choose whom they will hire. In good times, if they have ten things they are looking for, they may select someone with only six or seven because no one is available. During bad times the exact opposite is true.

Changing a career is even more difficult. People have established a certain salary and standard of living. Unless, they are financially independent, making a career change can be costly. Companies usually don't want to hire someone they know does not have the experience or training accumulated throughout the years.

The best way to orchestrate a career change is to do it in the company where you are currently working. They know you and, hopefully, you have developed a positive relationship with your peers, superiors, and subordinates. You are a known quantity and don't present the risk an outsider would.

The problem here is how do you get the support of your current boss? The last thing you want is to have this person angry and not in your corner. Unless you are invited to make this desired change, which rarely happens, you need to proceed slowly and with caution.

This may require a certain amount of behavior that is viewed as just common curiosity. Get to know people in your company who are in the career field you are interested in. Start to hang out with them for an occasional coffee, lunch, or other kind of get together. Find out what they like and dislike about their job. Are there a lot of requirements such as overtime, weekend work, or take-home work?

Are they growing or contracting and why?

If they are growing, this can be a possible opportunity. If they are stable and someone has been recruited away or is retiring, this could be another opportunity. Do you really have the experience and training to do this job? Are there outside certificates or specific classes you need to take to even qualify at the entry level?

Regardless, changing careers within the company you are with is almost always the better way to go. There are times when doing this is not an option and you have to go outside of the company. The problems you need to address are twofold: First, you and your work habits/abilities can only be determined by reference checks for a new company. Secondly, since this is going to be a new career, there is risk involved by the hiring officer that you may find you don't like, or other issues such as your abilities don't match, the learning curve is long, or productivity may take months or years, and the list can be longer than you will be able to tolerate.

The person doing the hiring has to be able and want to take a major risk. More often than not, this means you may have to find a friend, family member, or prior associate who will be willing to hire you into a new role. This can often take a lot of networking and searching to find.

Chances are almost non-existent that a career change will be found through a search firm—contingency or retained. Search firms are used by corporations to find people in a given field who can hit the ground running and require little or no training. Often, companies engage the service of these firms because they can pull someone from a direct competitor. This way the person being hired knows vital information such as the product(s), suppliers, competitors, buyers, and major company concerns. A month after someone from a direct competitor starts, they are probably at 80 percent or above in productivity.

Most people seeking jobs would like someone to find one for them. It is often referred to as the "I want to be asked to dance" syndrome. Professionals in the recruiting industry are not going to be there to do this, as previously noted. People who will do this will be people who know you very well and consider you a friend or very close colleague.

There may be more people in your network who will reach out and help than a decade ago. They want to do you a favor in hopes you will keep them on your "A list" and return the favor when they have similar needs. Most people recognize that jobs, companies, and careers are changing/disappearing at an accelerated rate. The most shock and sometimes slow learning comes from those who have been somewhere for five or more years.

Those who have been in this boat have often had to work long days and weekends. Frequently, and regrettably, they have not networked much outside their work environment. When you are putting in fifty or more hours a week—as many, if not most, are doing today—it is harder to maintain an outside network. Yet, this is more valuable than the corporate job.

"Hitting the bricks" after five or more years at the same organization creates a very confused and puzzled candidate. Things have changed significantly since the last time they sought work and there is a learning process. Technology alone now changes every six to nine months, when a few years ago it was eighteen. If the company you worked for hadn't kept up, or couldn't afford to, the new job seeker can be lost in both job and new career search.

Off shoring has been going on for decades. Those who don't believe need only to try to find something made in the country where they live. Even this can be a moving target. Suppliers change for many reasons such as the cost of a product. This may shift as new providers from other countries enter the market. A natural disaster such as floods or earthquakes can quickly switch providers in almost an instant and without notice.

People coming into the market or changing careers

find the suppliers and business contacts at this current company are different than the new company's they are talking with. This can be a very important part of one's research before interviewing. If your current company does a lot of business in China and Germany, what if the company you now have under consideration deals with Japan and Korea?

Those entering the job market or seeking a career change must do extensive research before talking to potential future employers. You don't want to shoot any silver bullets before you know what is going on in the market you are now entering. Also, you want to research every company before talking with them, so you don't over-shoot or totally miss their expectations.

Also, there are good companies and bad companies, so you need to do your homework. The last thing you want to do is join a company that has had three to six people in the position you are looking at in the last few years. "Churn-and-burn" companies are almost always in the market for new and often unsuspecting people.

Here is the problem: People want to believe they are different and it won't happen to them. Whenever possible, you want to talk to the last couple of people who held the position you are looking at. Ask about the corporate culture, the people you will be working for and with, and why the position is vacant. This can help you avoid walking into a no-win situation.

Check out the company's finances and its standing with competitors. The last thing you want to do is sign on with a company that may go bankrupt and/or have its senior executive team asked to leave.

It may also be a great company and well managed, but soon to be sold or merged. The company that is bought or is at the bottom end of a merger usually will lose most of its employees. The one on the lower end of these events often sheds up to 90 percent of its employees after the transaction is completed.

If you are part of a group that is retained, will you be relocated? Even huge companies that are bought by other large out-of-state companies often don't remain in place. The functions and often some of the remaining people are moved to the new owner's other location(s).

Chapter 7
Staying Current

Rapid change is the norm in today's business world, not the exception. The worst thing that can happen is getting buried in a company's corporate culture. One day you wake up and find the corporation and your job is gone. The new world you are thrown into is completely different than what you know or had previously learned.

Knowing the job market is always valuable whether you are looking for a new job, career change, or mistakenly thinking you are in a secure position. Economic conditions can change very rapidly. In today's world economy, what happens in France or Greece can significantly affect jobs in China or the United States.

It is not just global economics that can be influenced, but weather, earthquakes, and wars can put one out of work when least expected. The earthquake and tsunami that badly damaged Japan had a significant effect on companies and jobs around the world. Auto manufacturers, competitor manufacturers, and so on in a wide range of countries were directly affected when they couldn't get parts that were manufactured in the disaster area. This, of course, extended to suppliers and dealers, as well as manufacturers for obvious reasons.

When dramatic events occur, knowing your company or organization very well can help you survive the coming changes. If you were with an auto manufacturer when the disaster hit Japan, did you know how much dependence your company had on their parts? Were there possible supplies from other countries? What is your stock on hand situation?

Cultivating good sources of information within your current organization—or organizations, if you are simultaneously with more than one—can be invaluable. Usually, close sources in finance and in sales can be very valuable. Your finance contacts can tell you if it appears that revenue is okay, the numbers are being met, the line of credit is secure, and so on. Those in sales can often give you some advance knowledge if a major client is leaving, if sales are down for any number of reasons, or the revenues of both of these. This insight into the company can help you on a lot of fronts regarding what may occur in the future.

Privately owning a few shares of a public company you work for can also be of value. You probably want to do this in a very small amount outside of purchases through the company's internal 401K or other related corporate programs. This may enhance your ability to find out from street sources about profitability issues, pending lawsuits, tax problems, and issues with government regulators, and so on. The more accurate and less corporate controlled your information is, the more prepared you can be for what may happen to you.

I mentioned earlier about professional organizations related to your job and company. These can be invaluable and provide a wide range of helpful information to help you prepare for changes. People have found out from colleagues in these groups that their company is quietly under the radar seeking suitors to buy or merge with them. Some have even found through these groups that a search firm is quietly looking for someone to fill the job they currently hold. These are probably not pleasant bits of information, but ones that allow them to plan and prepare.

Working hard at what you do and being the top performer used to generate one's security in these jobs. This is no longer the case. In fact, prepare to be where you are currently at no more than a few years, if that. You can be performing at a fantastic level and the company appears to be growing and expanding rapidly. The better the company is doing the more they become a target for acquisition. Once your company is acquired it is only a matter of time, usually a year or less, before your job may disappear.

What does this mean to employees? In today's world the most successful people are always in a job search. The only real loyalty people should have is to themselves and their networks because chances are that a current company will only be a vague memory in five to ten years.

Smart people use their current company as it uses them—for their future benefit and career development. Many organizations pay for professional memberships, pay people for travel to enhance their job knowledge, and even pay employees for trips to do company-related speaking engagements. Companies want their names and image out in front of the public, so because you are their emissary it is a win-win situation.

Getting on the speaking circuit as a guest speaker can be one of the best career development and career information resources one can have or ever achieve. You say you are, "Terrified of public speaking." Honestly, we all are even professional speakers. Most people have methods to cope with this fear and even use it to their advantage.

The best way, and truly another source of valuable contacts, is "Toastmasters (mentioned several times in prior chapters)" or a related group of people who get together on a regular basis to work to overcome their fear of being in front of a group. They help in this way as well as to expand each other's network. Always keep in mind the old adage, "You can't be too rich, too thin, or know too many people!"

The author developed a fear of groups as he approached early middle age—period when many of us lose some of the bravado we acquired early in life; we look back and take inventory of missed opportunities. A contact, mentor, and wise advisor/mentor said that he had overcome some—it never completely goes away—fear of public speaking by teaching in the evening extension college system.

This had a multiple advantages. It provided some extra income, was a little less fear provoking because the audiences were younger, less experienced, and it got the speaker's name out there. This is a hard combination to beat. You can also use it to practice some techniques or ideas you may try in the future with peers or subordinates to see what works. It gives you a comfort level you haven't or won't have in normal circumstances. This said, it has been noted multiple times that classroom teaching may be going away.

In the classroom you are in charge and, if you are having a difficult day in the speaking arena, you can quickly remove the pressure. You will find you can adjust assignments quickly by having the students speak on what they think about the current classroom topics under consideration. You are no longer the speaker but a moderator, which on a bad day can be much less stressful.

Getting colleagues to come in as guest speakers for thirty to sixty minutes has multiple advantages: First, the students love to hear guest speakers, and your teaching ratings will rise. Secondly, those invited to speak will be flattered and you will become a more senior contact in their network.

You also get to see the various techniques, ideas, and speaking patterns these people have. It is a very good time to creatively select items they use that you are comfortable with and that you can use. In a ten- or twelve-session course you can easily bring in five or six guest speakers without it being overkill. Each one will bring something to the table and you will have a wide selection.

People who are guests often prepare extensively for the thirty to sixty minutes they are given. This means they bring some of their best material and often some of the latest and state-of-the-art handouts. This can be very, very valuable for you! They have "cherry picked" from their background to try to ensure they do a great job in a limited time.

A verbal request will never get you the type of information you can glean from a time-limited guest speaker. They are going to pack years of knowledge into the brief time they are allowed.

Much of what they share from the podium can be taken by you and used in future speaking engagements you do. Being an observer in the room gives you the latitude to observe what works and doesn't work. You are not the one on the stage, so you can observe the faces and reactions of the audience—your students. This is also a time you may wish to take notes yourself. If a particular joke, subject, or bit of information, gets a positive response from the audience, write it down. You want to create a list of things that worked, as these are ones you will want to try yourself in the future.

Many people teach classes related to what they do in their corporate job. Your guest speakers can also provide you with valuable work-related information they would normally zealously guard. Remember, they are trying to impress the audience with the latest information available to them. You may be a competitor, but their main concerns when "on stage" is to win the group's approval.

The author is engaged in retained executive search and sponsors numerous group events. He invites other search executives who are direct competitors as speakers. Yes, there is potential for loss of business doing this, but the knowledge gained is believed to far out weigh any loss. Does this mean taking away competitors' clients? Probably not.

The real value is hearing them express what fields they see for future business, how the economy is affecting them, and what techniques they find of value. In many cases it reinforces what you already know, but there are always some new tidbits you didn't know or hadn't thought about. These can be very valuable.

Chapter 8
Career Obsolescence

Decades ago a person could select a career field he or she found of interest. The next step was to get the necessary training such as college, technical school, apprenticeship, and then move forward doing what the person had chosen. In past decades, this might be someone's chosen field for life. This, unfortunately, is no longer true.

Think about having a young person approach you and ask, "What is a good field to choose?" Take a step back and ask yourself what you might have answered five years ago. It is probably not the same response you would give today. Will today's answer sustain the next five years?

Technology is moving forward at an accelerated rate and people are changing jobs right and left. Have you even seen an assembly line today? Most of them are filled with machines doing the work technicians used to do. Try talking face-to-face with a teenager today. It is hard to get teenagers to stop texting long enough to carry on a short conversation.

These changes are accelerating at an alarming pace. People are walking around with handheld devices and some are even implanting buzzer systems under their skin so they know when a call comes in. We are not too far off from having something like a contact lens so we can be on a system without worrying about carrying a device. Wearable technology is already here. One in ten US adults (according to some statistics) now owns a fitness tracker. This wearable device will gain over the next several years as people switch from tablet and mobile devices to smaller wearable technologies that can provide the same or enhanced function. Starting recently the revenue that wearable technology will gain during the next five years is predicted to raise 40 percent as consumers switch from tablet and mobile devices to smaller wearable technologies that can provide the same apps.

We may not like these changes, but they are a fact. Technology will change today's jobs and create new ones. Part of the process is staying current with these changes and being on the leading edge to take advantage of them. Doing this can be a challenge.

The world economy also makes future work an issue. CEOs of major and minor companies don't hesitate to send jobs to other countries where salaries are lower and potential profits are higher. It is not uncommon to see hundreds or even thousands of jobs disappearing overnight as they are outsourced to different countries. Simultaneously, workers in this country who had these jobs are laid off.

Working in a government job — city, county, state, federal — used to be almost a choice of last resort. Currently, it is probably the most sought-after opportunity. Jobs in this category are probably not going to be off-shored by some gazillion-dollar corporate CEO who is vacationing most of the year.

There are still government layoffs, but they don't occur totally and without lengthy warning. They also provide protected benefits and pensions. Most corporations have done away with any real pension systems and have moved people into high-fee 401K plans, which are often called a "defined contribution plan." There are real corporate pension plans called "defined benefit plans," but these become targets during any form of revenue loss, downsizing, and so on.

Working for a government entity may offer some of the security that is no longer available in a corporate environment. Even more important, it may give you needed time to explore where you want to go to look for a new job. Chances are you will not be working extremely long days and weekends just to keep your job.

Often there are internal sources you can contact to explore careers in other fields that might be of interest to you. In a government job, your feet aren't constantly in the fire to produce ever-increasing amounts and the hours worked are usually reasonable. This gives you an opportunity to look around and think, talk, and explore the direction things are taking.

Secondly, if change does take place, your opportunity to get in and be trained in the change process exists. People without the new state-of-the-art skills will more likely be laid off or moved to the side in corporate. New people with these skills will be immediately brought in to do the work. This not only speeds up the process, but significantly cuts the cost of training or retraining. Government employers will be slower to act and more likely to do the required training of existing workers.

Of course, there are two sides to this. The government may not be as quick to embrace the new technology or changes taking place. It may have to be tried, proven, and totally accepted before it is going to be made. Consequently, the workers may not be on the leading edge.

This can create two groups of government workers: Those who like what they are doing and will be somewhat protected as things change and those who want something different than they are currently doing. Chances are the government is not going to provide classes to help people identify what they like doing best. Again, this puts people on their own to identify what makes them happy.

More and more people are turning to outside resources to identify this. Many professional organizations are finding this a topic of interest that draws large numbers of members to meetings. Even people who think they are happy in their present line of work will come to explore and discover if they have other avenues of interest. There are truly very few who are absolutely positive that what they are doing is the only way to go.

There are a wide range of outside resources one can go to for help. The issue here is both trust and cost. As previously noted, there are strong providers in this area and weak ones. Like any other service there are just plain charlatans out there looking to make a quick buck. This re-emphasizes the importance of one's network. Here people can talk to people they know and trust about their own career analysis. This will include the pluses and minuses of using a specific career counselor.

Let's say you have identified someone who you want to consider giving you career help and advice. They provide you with references. Are they references from people in your field? If not, why not? It could be that the outside counselor has experience, but not in your field. Most of us want someone who knows our field very well and maybe even did the exact job we are currently doing.

Once you think you have a person who seems to be a good career counselor/guide, how many people in your network know and have used him or her? There are many online networking groups you can use for your inquiries. The one thing to keep in mind consistently through the counselor hiring process is: do you know the person giving the reference and is it someone you trust?

Picking the right time to start a new career is just as important. This is often a major income source and is important not only to your happiness and sense of survival, but to pay for necessities. Again, the last one in is often the first one out. How secure is the area and organization you are going to be entering? Where is it in the realm of state-of-the art technology?

The last thing you want is to go into something you love and find out it is a function the organization questions. Even worse is finding out the organization and its leaders are not highly valued and may not be there in the long term.

It is your life and your job. We spend probably two thirds of our waking hours either working or thinking about our work. Most people will spend six figures on where they live, even though most of the time in their private home they are sleeping. Getting a car we like can consume thirty or more thousand dollars. We research and shop for our houses and our cars. Many check limited resources when considering a job at a new company.

Too many people just fall into a job without thinking, checking, looking, comparing. Spending thousands of dollars finding the right fit is often out of the question. Even spending a few hundred is often not a consideration. If you take a step back and think about it, the work you do will capture most of your waking hours. It will not be your home or your car. Strange, isn't it?

What about finding the work we love to do?

Taking a step back, we may want to consider the time and cost of doing/purchasing some serious career coaching/counseling. Psychological testing on our likes and dislikes can bring some significant ah-ha moments, or "I never thought about that." The results can sometimes be dramatic and both personally and financially rewarding — if we are careful and do our research on those we select to help us. This may be even more valuable than the same work we do to find a house or a car. In fact, we may be able to develop a job that allows us significantly more money to purchase the other things we value so highly.

Chapter 9
Job Obsolescence

One of the first things one should understand in finding a new or different job is the fact that the job market is not constant during the year. There are definitely windows of opportunity and then there are periods when hardly anything is happening. They tend to follow the same pattern in good times and in bad. The only difference will be in volume during a growth cycle or during a recession.

The big window opens about January fifteenth and goes until June fifteenth. There is not an exact figure, but more than 60 percent of all hiring is done during this period. Things then slow down after the middle of June and come to almost a complete stop during July and August. It takes many people in most organizations to approve a new hire and many of the decision makers are on vacation.

The author was in the outplacement business for many years helping people who were trying to find jobs. Most of these people had full office support paid for by their prior employers. The standing joke among those in outplacement was even in fantastic economic times during the summer you almost had to nail the windows shut if you were in a high rise building. Things go almost totally black during July and August. People looking for jobs get literally terrified because everything seems to dry up.

A small window opens around the second or third week of September and goes until Thanksgiving week—barring a major catastrophic event such as 9/11. When this occurred, the little window never opened. Other activities such as government shutdowns can cause hiring to cease for a period of time.

After Thanksgiving week, things tend to go black until January 15. One observer joked and called it the "silly season." His comment was that a large portion of the senior staff was not there because it is a popular time for vacation or holiday reasons. He went on to state that those who were there were too drunk or hung over and didn't get much done.

All joking aside, this is a period of slow hiring for a number of reasons. The primary one is that those who are hired need to be trained and brought fully into the new work culture. Many experienced people are not available for the reasons mentioned. In fact, some organizations close down toward the end of December and don't re-open until after the first of the year.

New employees during this period of time don't have the training available during more active times of the year. Companies may also incur added expenses if they just hire someone and then give him or her paid leave for plant closures. Even if offices remain open, there are multiple paid days off during this period to respect the holiday season and many companies see this as a waste of time.

Interestingly, this may not be as true for someone wanting to change jobs or careers. It takes usually a minimum of six weeks to launch a search. The downtime periods between the big and little windows may be excellent times to get your job search package together such as a current resume, LinkedIn profile, list of companies of interest, network contacts, and career interest tests.

The people who are working during these slow times aren't as hard pressed or harried. They often have more uninterrupted time to talk. The downtime between windows is significant; it occurs during months. It may take more effort on the seeker's part to reach the person of interest, but it can be done. Those who are there will often spend more time with you.

There are usually circumstances and technology changes that alert us to prepare for a new job or a major change in the existing job. You don't have to look very far to find these and you will always see many people in the organization who are in total denial of what is going on. They are making no preparation for the career "train wreck" that some others excluding them see coming.

A good example is the postal service. During many, many decades this has been an area where people could find a job, work, and eventually get a nice retirement with excellent benefits. The computer came along and e-mail, texting, tweeting, started replacing handwritten communication. What was the solution? Increase postage rates to make up for the lost revenue! Really? Increased rates just accelerated the change. More and more people switch to other sources, even some who would have continued if the rates had not increased.

A good example of this change is the promotion of online banking by the major financial institutions. They are constantly advertising and verbally coaxing customers to switch to doing their banking online. It saves the bank significant money to handle debits and credits online versus in person or particularly by way of regular mail. Most major recipients of checks such as the gas company, department of water and power, credit card companies all direct deposit the checks they receive. They would rather have customers allow them to set up an online payment system than mail a check.

Stockholders quickly find companies trying to get them involved in online activity, from voting to the mailing of annual reports. This is an expensive process when you consider the weight of most annual reports. There are large sums of money involved and most companies would require investors to switch to online, if they could do so legally.

Everything from reading books to viewing news, making stock transactions, viewing movies is changing. Many people are now shopping online. These changes are wreaking havoc with companies and sales tax collectors. It used to be that you walked into a store made a purchase and (depending on the state, city), and you paid a tax. This has changed rapidly with the ability to buy online and many were saving money. Government has been rushing to close this revenue loss and it will quickly disappear. This is a two-edged sword because there is a delivery component to this type of shopping. There are also the concerns for commercial space since some corporations are finding they don't have to build or pay rent if they go online.

This goes back to some of the earlier comments about computer systems themselves. The obsolescence rate is increasing. What used to take eighteen months has been reduced significantly. The rate has dropped to a fraction of this number and will continue to do so.

There is always concern with the cost of the instruments/ equipment one uses. Then there is how much you spend to backup the system in case of a loss or crash. Trying to decide the options and the pluses and minuses in this area can be mind boggling; and whatever method chosen will be criticized.

Of course, these are only some of the problems and related expenses. Will the networks you belong to for social and/or business purposes also have cost implications? Everyone is out to make money. Some of the very popular and valuable sites are free, but charge a fee to upgrade. Paying to upgrade may be valuable depending on how it is used. This can change, and knowing when to drop the upgrade can be as much of a challenge as choosing to use it to begin with.

Being on a networking or social site such as LinkedIn or Facebook, has certain effects on people that they need to be aware of. A major one is and always will be security. This comes in a wide range of concerns and issues. One is how safe is your information from prying eyes? Whom do you want to be able to see your data, identify you, contact you, or know where you live?

Women, older people, and the disabled may have serious concerns about their physical safety. The author is aware of colleagues who have posted vacation plans and shared information on times and dates involved. They then returned to find their homes had been robbed and now are much more cautious about who they tell and where their schedule is displayed.

There is the old adage about "an ounce of image is worth a pound of performance." This is very, very true about all the sites we choose to be on. In the executive search business, we find clients going to LinkedIn while we are on the phone with them and looking at a mentioned candidate's profile. Just mentioning a person's name will often cause this to happen, even before we have the chance to forward a resume.

What does this say? It means that someone's LinkedIn profile may be just as important and maybe more important than the resume since it may create that all important first impression. This may cause many people to be careful about the appearance of this document in all facets. The author has more than fifty recommendations, but only posts seven to keep it short and easy to read. The more a profile looks like a two-page resume, the better.

Care needs to be taken on all sites—both business

and those purely social—so nothing negative is viewed. Companies review social sites as well to be sure these don't reveal ethical, moral, or illegal behavior. Stay away from anything on the Internet that shows things like drinking, partying, sexual behavior, etc. If you wouldn't want the picture flashed on the screen during a staff meeting, don't post it!

We can probably never address all the Internet concerns, but protecting data from scammers or from total loss during a computer crash is another major concern. This can be tough to control, but something to discuss with your computer support expert to minimize problems and worries. I use the word "minimize" because they will never be eliminated. All one has to do is look at the corporate and government systems that get hacked despite billions of dollars of protection. The average person cannot even come close to this type of protection.

Chapter 10
Career Changes

The first place most people go to when they decide they want to find a new job or are laid off is a search firm. This is probably not a good idea. Those directly approaching search firms who actually get a position this way is estimated by the author, who is in the business, to probably be less than 2 percent—not very good odds.

People want to go to search firms because they mistakenly believe search firms find positions for job seekers. In fact, search firms find people for client companies and there is a very, very big difference. Also, people don't want to work at finding a job. What they really want is to sit back and have someone do the work at little or no cost to them because they are so fantastic.

Let's take a step back and look at search firms. There are retained firms who are hired by companies who pay a significant amount of money upfront and most out-of-pocket expenses for the firm to find candidates for them. They normally go to a firm like this when they have found their own internal sources and outside contacts can't deliver. In some cases, there is an incumbent they want to get rid of, but the position is so valuable that they need an outsider to confidentially fly under the radar and find the person. This way they will not fire the current employee until his or her replacement is able to start. Since they are paying a substantial amount, they often want someone from a direct competitor.

The next step down is contingency search firms. They only get paid when the candidate they submit is hired by the client. Usually, they are given a list of six to eight qualifications prospective candidates must have before they want to see a resume. Experienced clients know that since the search firm receives no money until the person is hired it may have to give the assignment to multiple firms. They usually continue searching through their own networks preferring always to use this source, since they will not have to pay any fees.

One of the reasons companies may give the search to multiple contingency firms is that they may not spend the time on a search as retained search firms do. Why? Contingency firms only get paid when one of their candidates is hired. They may work on a search for a limited period of time based on their probability of success and getting the fee. As soon as an easier search appears, some may drop what they are doing and go after it. Now, this is not always true. Some contingency firms want a strong long-term client relationship. They will put in the extra effort to make the client happy, so they will get future work.

When working with a contingency firm as a candidate, unless you are almost an identical match to the multiple criteria the hiring firm gives the search firm, you are not going to be called back. Many candidates become very angry when these calls are not returned. The probability is they are just not a match for the search or any others the search firm is working on.

Those seeking a job need to know that they may have little or no knowledge of the current job market. Too many people do very little networking until they are out of work. Basically, they just focus on the company they work for and their colleagues within the company. When the ax falls, they are in an entirely new world that they are totally unfamiliar with. Many have limited outside contacts and they don't even have a current resume or any current interviewing skills.

Those who are fortunate enough will have company-paid outplacement services from a major firm in the outplacement industry. Many senior managers and executives have this service written into their Letter of Agreement before even joining a company. This is a very wise move and it is a form of insurance when one is let go. Some companies provide this service almost automatically, but the level of service can vary by a wide range of circumstances such as the company's financial strength or level of position.

Why is this so valuable? The major firms in the outplacement or career transition business have worked with thousands of people who have been terminated or let go. They know that people who go through the process are dealing with emotional issues such as the loss of a loved one, a divorce, or separation from a significant other. The experts often say people in this area go through DABDA which stands for Disbelief, Anger, Bargaining, Depression and, finally, Acceptance.

In fact, those terminated will cycle through this process many, many times. Here an experienced guide can help people deal with major trauma. They explain to the new job seeker that what he or she is feeling is normal and to recognize rather than deny it.

A person can't focus on the efforts needed to find a new job until he or she deals with the DABDA experience. It is not something that goes away. An experienced job counselor will work through this in the beginning with a person who has had the loss. Counselors will normally tell people in this kind of situation to set aside ten minutes or so each day to go through this process, and then drop it for the rest of the day and focus on finding a new job. This way they can deal with their feelings, but put their effort where it needs to be.

A good counselor will help people understand the current job market, focus on their resume, expanding their networks, practicing interviewing—even videotaping with feedback—updating online profiles, and more. These are all things someone coming out of corporate may know little or nothing about. Going into a job search is a whole new world for most people.

There is a real red flag if a company does not provide outplacement or career services to the leaving/laid off employee. Remember, people don't know how to go through the very difficult process of leaving or how to find a new job. In fact, most terminated people want someone to do the work for them—someone who can pick and choose throughout multiple job/position opportunities.

There are various scam artists who know this and take advantage of people at this very vulnerable time. Many major outplacement or career transition firms will not take payment from an individual and will only accept money from the corporate sponsor who let the individual go. Many of the outplacement firms have this restriction.

This means that someone who is let go and not given outplacement by their corporations cannot usually hire a major outplacement firm. People always need it, but they have to be very, very cautious if they are going to personally buy it. There are some firms and experienced individuals who can provide this service and will take payment from individuals. Simultaneously, this is an area that attracts a wide variety of "scam artists."

If you are let go from a company and it doesn't provide outplacement/career transition services, proceed with caution. This is not to say a person should not move on and not get help. Almost all people leaving a corporate environment need a career counselor. If paying for it themselves, they must check, double check, and even triple check the background of the person or organization they are planning to use. In a way, it is a lot like selecting someone to manage your personal finances—you can't be too careful!

One possible source might be to talk with some of the top outplacement/career transition firms even though they won't take money from an individual. Explain your situation, explain that you know they can only work for or accept money from corporations, and ask who they would recommend as a private source you can use. In fact, you might do this with several of these leading outplacement firms. Then, fully reference check the person or firm being recommended.

It was noted earlier that companies are constantly coming and going. Even the largest ones don't last forever and this change is happening at an accelerated rate. Size and a company's age no longer equates to a long-term existence in today's world. In fact, it may mean just the opposite.

Check your network to see who in your area of interest has recently started a company. The smaller entrepreneurial companies can sometimes be more visible and transparent in both what they are doing and their place in the market. This gives you the advantage, with the rapid changes in technology, of identifying a position that may offer substantial future growth and opportunity.

Getting in early can enhance your own personal skill base. You will be in a learning mode and dealing with the most current changes and developments. This also may provide an opportunity to get an early valuable ownership position, preferably stock related rather than a direct ownership that could expose your personal assets.

In today's world almost no one can plan on receiving a corporate pension. The best most can do is roll over related 401K plans as company changes occur. However, many people are carving out a nice financial niche by getting early stock options related to a new and growing company. If this company grows and is sold or does an initial public offering (IPO), you can come away in a very good position financially. Some people even find they get enough in this situation that having to work in the future becomes an option and not a necessity.

The tech industry is one group of companies where this opportunity is significant. The reasons for this may include: it is not heavily dependent on materials, manufacturing space, heavy duty tools, and more. Many of the startups in the tech area even require little or no office space.

Those who are able to identify these firms focus on where most future growth will be. It should be a constant target that everyone has on his or her list. Ringing the bell in this area can provide you with significant career growth, financial rewards, and future security.

Chapter 11
Relocation and Fast Growing Areas

We all know things change in this world. Sometimes it is over time and other times very rapidly. It wasn't too long ago when Detroit was a dynamic city and the center of auto production in the United States. Now, Detroit is a collapsing area. Blocks of abandoned houses and commercial properties are bulldozed away to try to remove some of the major blight and deterioration that has hit the area.

Los Angeles used to be the hub of the aerospace industry. Many of the companies are gone. This said, there are still many aerospace sub-contractors in the area. Entertainment is still a major player, but the real driving force currently seems to be companies in the tech area.

There are many cities across the country that are at both at the very high end and the very low end of the hiring/growth cycle. Remember this book is being written about the topic the author speaks on. Detroit is mentioned because it is currently not doing well, but it is where the author was born. Los Angeles is currently at the high end and is doing very well. It is currently where the author lives and works. These two are used as examples, but there might be better ones.

This makes several points of concern whenever anyone is considering moving to a new location. Areas go up and they come down. Depending on the industry diversification in an area it can result in huge changes in employment and home values. We all need to look at this factor in relocation consideration. The last thing anyone wants is to buy somewhere new and in time find out they have lost their job and their home has lost a huge portion of its original value.

One thing many people don't factor in with relocation is what it will do to their network. Many, even fantastic networkers, don't stray too far from home. In any relocation, your most valuable asset—your network—will suffer. How quickly you can re-build and re-establish can vary both by the location chosen and the person's skill set in networking.

There are professional groups that require a prior background history with them before you can be truly accepted. In some areas you can be there for decades and still be considered somewhat of a newcomer. This can affect you if all of a sudden a job you have goes away. Most people need a close knit network at these times.

People often forget to factor in their lifestyle when relocating. Different areas have different views on what is considered an acceptable lifestyle.

The author once did a search to fill an executive position in a very isolated island community. Research indicated one of the major activities in this community was gossip. It was quickly noted that what happened in a person's personal life during a weekend could become almost "front page news" the next week.

What does this have to do with relocation? Truly, it had a lot of do with it. The people being considered not only had to be able to deal with an isolated environment, but they had to have very austere personal lives. An executive who liked to party, was an occasional heavy drinker, a swinger, used recreational drugs, was a fast driver had to be ruled out. Even those with too strong and open religious values might be cause for upset. The chosen candidates could neither be bad or too good, but had to border on almost boring. Lots of people think about everything but lifestyle when considering relocation. This can be dangerous if you don't have an experienced expert in the equation to guide you. The last thing you want is to relocate and then find out you don't fit in with your neighbors or the community as a whole.

You normally can't take much of your network with you when you relocate. In certain instances, if you are with a major organization and are moving to a division in a different area, this may save pieces of it. A totally new company hundreds or thousands of miles from where you previously were is a different story.

Let's take a look at both of these occurrences, since each may have some different components. Transferring with a company you have been part of for years means you already have a certain number of trusted sources and contacts. It may also free up some additional time to work on expanding your new local external network. Why? As an experienced member of an existing company, you don't have to learn a completely new corporate culture. Companies/organizations are a lot like individuals and they all have their own rules, values, likes and dislikes, product lines, and customers. I could easily go on for pages about these.

Certainly, when you transfer with an existing company, there are going to be new elements such as names, faces, office locations, phone extensions, and a parking space. Simultaneously, you are not starting from ground zero because it is in a division of one you had worked with and will generally have the same corporate/organization "personality." Your prior work with them will allow you greater ease in sorting out major issues and not stepping on corporate "land mines." Before you even fully accepted the transfer, you used your internal sources to scope out what you are really getting into and what to expect.

This means you will have more time to try to work on the other aspect of networking—rebuilding your professional network in the new community. This is always a major portion of your life line in your career. Superstars throw themselves into this almost immediately.

There is still a vast amount of effort that has to go into this. You have to identify appropriate professional organizations you will need to attend. Many times ones you belonged to at your prior location will have a local chapter, so you can transfer. This does not mean you won't have to earn the respect and trust of the new people, but it does give you an easier start.

Also, the value of a professional organization can vary significantly from area to area. An organization that was a key player in one area is not necessarily so in another and vice versa. In essence, this is another area one needs to quickly scope out. You may find new professional groups you did not know existed are what run your current area. Again, be they old or new professional groups, you need to get onboard and earn their respect and acceptance.

This is often done by volunteering to chair or lead activities, being a speaker, making monetary contributions, and more. Regardless of other priorities in your life, nothing is more important than re-establishing your network.

The worst case scenario is usually having to relocate to a new company. Not only do you lose your outside network, but you have to re-establish yourself in an entirely new corporate environment and culture. Obviously, to avoid losing your job, the internal focus must have priority. With a little luck, possibly some people from prior work lives may also have joined this company before you and can provide some insight into your new world, which can help a little.

There is usually a new employee orientation system where the "newbies" are brought in by HR and shown things such as org charts, product samples, corporate brochures, executive profiles, and summary business plans.

However, one of the most important aspects is the visions/policies existing in almost every organization, which can be forbidden to be shared. These can be vital things no one dares to mention such as a low level employee who has a romantic relationship with the company president or maybe the apprentice who is the niece/nephew of the COO. These folks may be low in the structure because of their current title/work level in the organization, but they have unbelievable power. Make the mistake of crossing one of these and you will be out the door before you know what has hit you. These issues fly under the radar and should be at the top of items discussed in orientation, but often don't even dare be mentioned. HR certainly isn't going to go near them. Most orientations are very conservative—the topics of very real importance are off limits and never mentioned.

So professionals smile, go through the formal orientation, and then focus on finding out what is really going on. All organizations have what are often referred to as "corporate mouths." These are people, usually long-term employees, who love to gossip. The first thing a new person needs to do is identify who they are and very quickly spend time with them.

One way to find these resources is to casually mention to colleagues in your department an interest in knowing who the "gossip mongers" are and verify it. Once identified you want to arrange a breakfast, lunch, or a drink, with these folks. It is usually wise to do this off premises and in a private environment—just you and the individual. Just a coffee together in-house or a lunch meeting in the cafeteria may not be comfortable enough for them to truly open up. The best time-tested method is to get them to go out for drinks and you buy. A little alcohol goes a long way in getting them to open up completely about who is doing what to whom and how often. These meetings are ten times more valuable than any corporate orientation.

The experience of "on boarding" with a new company is always exhausting. People are usually exhausted by the end of the first three weeks. There is what is often called the "new employee flu" that hits normally in the third or fourth week and can often mimic the symptoms of real flu. Since the person is new, he or she does not want to take time off and must struggle through taking handfuls of various pain and cold remedies.

If we then put a change in companies with relocation, this just adds to the stress. Most people need several months—sometimes six months to a year—before they feel comfortable with their new environment.

This means there are several things to ask for before accepting the change. One might be a gradual move where you are provided pay for lodging for the first year at the new location and regular paid travel back and forth. Your family can remain in their current location for at least a year and you can visit them on a regular basis, paid for by the new company. There are all kinds of variations of this that can be included in this option and you want to scope them all out and discuss them with friends and colleagues who have extensive relocation experience.

There are other alternatives that should be considered that includes possibly a hiring agreement clause that provides a full relocation expense coverage back to your place of origin should your job go away in the first two or three years. Remember, one of the major targets you are trying to protect is your network. In relocating to a new company a certain amount of time has to be spent focusing on the new corporate environment. There will be a certain amount of delay in working on one's outside network, which is very important and puts another risk factor in the equation.

Let's say a person has relocated, gotten fully on board with his or her current position and then gets laid off. Often this is a very real consideration in light of the "last one in, first one out" adage. This can truly create a catastrophe because now not only are you without a job, but you have incurred moving expenses, possibly a new mortgage, and much more. Worst of all, you are now living in an environment where your external network is almost non-existent.

This is a major consideration that many overlook when moving to a new company. It probably should be at the top of the list and one of the things you want to consider in negotiations before you accept a position requiring you to relocate. There has to be time spent in the "on boarding" related to the company itself. This may take the better part of a year. Then you have to focus on building a new business/professional network outside the company in the new area. There is a tremendous amount of work involved in both the internal and external network building. Neither can be overlooked because your entire future depends on it!

Today we have an added item of focus. Most companies, large and small, are often involved in the international marketplace. This is relatively new having occurred in the last decade or so. This truly may broadly expand the networks one needs to service both internally and externally.

This is an issue that will continue to develop further over time. Many colleagues are now learning Chinese and it is becoming a major language of choice in the school systems. Selected consultants who travel frequently are also learning to speak the language to enhance their business potential. It will be interesting to see how this aspect of networking plays out over time. Many feel that China will be a major player in the future and that India will be an even stronger player. There is a broad range of futurists who feel India has much more in its favor in the coming decades. Only time will tell, to use an old cliché.

Chapter 12
Conclusion

We are all self-employed in today's world. Not only do jobs and companies come and go, but so do careers and employers. The days of getting trained/educated, learning the basics of the job, and working up the corporate ladder are over. This is not the way most people were brought up to believe and the concept is very difficult for a large part of the working population to accept.

Things that we once held dear such as a college education, now come into serious question. Many very, very successful people dropped out of college to pursue an area of interest that made them millionaires; Not sure, but some indicate this could include Steve Jobs and Bill Gates? These are two super stars and this is a real point if true. If they had continued in college, even pursued and completed degrees, it is debatable as to whether or not they would have succeeded as remarkably as they did. This concept is certainly not going to be embraced by educators who depend on the current system for their livelihood and well-being. If we take a step back and examine it, most of what a person learns in college as a college freshman and sophomore is obsolete by the time he or she is a junior or senior. Things continue to move ahead very rapidly and maybe obsolete more rapidly than anyone thinks possible. Could it be that the days of college being the stepping stone to the future are over?

Maybe we need to step back and look at our entire education system. Why isn't it currently working? What needs to change? How do we change it? How is the change going to be measured?

Today's work force must constantly step back and evaluate their skill set versus the current market and then take a second look at where the market will be in three to five years. Technology and related economic changes cause jobs and careers to come and go. A person may be doing fantastically today, but the entire environment he or she is in may not even exist in a few years. Education and learning are ongoing events and may be shorter and much more frequent than in the past. It is like a postal delivery person walking the streets delivering mail while talking and texting on his or her handheld device.

We can no longer depend on the education of the past, our current job, or our current employer. All are becoming obsolete at an accelerating rate. The only security we have is the one we develop ourselves.

The true security we have and that our very future depends on is our network. This should be everyone's focus, since in today's world it is how we control our destiny. Again, there are multiple networks in our daily lives coming from family, current work assignments, professional organizations, and every realm of life itself.

Again, getting back to the old adage, "You can't be too thin, too rich, or know too many people," we all for the most part, have to work for others. Even if we own the business, the customer is the boss. A very wise move is for every eight hours we spend doing something for the boss, we need to spend one hour doing something for ourselves.

This "something" is growing and building our network. It is an ongoing process, since people come and go in our lives. In fact, some will actually die and be gone for good. The others who remain have to constantly be evaluated and time spent on these is based on future value to us, both as individuals and as work-related contacts. Not only are we in a constant evaluation process, but a process of adding to our network on a regular basis. Taking a step back and looking at today's reality, in a truly successful day we have to make many additions to our network. Again, quality can be as important as quantity.

If we are focusing on a new skill set that will lead to future growth and/or work, this needs to be a target. We need to do things such as add people who are experienced in this area, we need to join professional organizations in this area, attend presentations about it, and possibly take a class (probably online) regarding it.

Networking is an art itself and we need to develop skills in the area on an ongoing basis. The past has indicated that a certain amount of face-to-face contact is invaluable. One face-to-face private meeting can be worth thirty phone calls or one hundred e-mails.

This, too, may be changing and some people feel "tweeting" is one of the most valuable ways to network. This extends to viewing people via videoconferencing and Skype. In fact, there are a wide range of new technologies on the horizon that may change/enhance the ability of face-to-face contact in a wide range of new ways via technology.

Regardless of what we think or value, the true way to control life is networking, networking, Networking. End of discussion!

Made in the USA
San Bernardino, CA
07 July 2017